Speak softly and laugh quietly

Also by Patrick Semple

A Parish Adult Education Handbook – Editor

Believe It Or Not – A Memoir

That Could Never Be – with K Dalton

The Rectory Dog – Poetry Collection

The Rector Who Wouldn't Pray For Rain – A Memoir

A Narrow Escape – Poetry Collection

Transient Beings – A Novel

Curious Cargo – A Travelogue

Being Published – A Creative Writing Guide

Slices of Life – A Collection of Short Stories

Nature's Playthings – A Novel

Another Slice – A Second Collection of Short Stories

Speak softly
and
laugh quietly

A collection of poetry and musings
by
Patrick Semple

Code Green Publishing

Copyright © 2020 by Patrick Semple

Patrick Semple asserts the moral right to be identified
as the author of this work.

A catalogue record for this book is available from the British Library.

ISBN 978-1-907215-25-4

Version 1.0

Cover design by Code Green Publishing

Published by
Code Green Publishing
Coventry, England

www.codegreenpublishing.com

Contents

Memory

Favoured Pieces

An all pervasive stillness.
Silent as the grave.
Each favoured piece
a memory for one now gone.

And so bereft,
all will be dispersed
to the four winds
and stand on merit alone.

Life goes on about its business
as the ocean closes over
a ship gone down.

Tegan

'Boo.' That's what they called you
when you were little more than just a speck.
And when you increased your Mummy's girth
they talked to you as though you were already here.
They stroked and soothed you and told you
how much they looked forward to your arrival.

Then you came
and all their pent up love enveloped you,
beautiful, miraculous little Boo.
When you were less than one hour old
your Dad held you to the window
and said: 'There's the world.'

It's out there that you'll grow up
and come to terms with all it means to be a part of it.
Meanwhile your Mum and Dad will make for you
your own small world filled with love.
Love, the best meaning, you will find,
that you can give to anything.

A Meeting

On a busy street I saw a face I knew I knew.
A man who'd been a boy at school.
We stopped and talked of childhood days.

I remembered much; he little.
He listened while I reminisced.
Nothing of what I said held interest.

I wondered what he'd done in life.
He didn't tell me and I didn't ask.

Going Back

Don't go back.
The years idealise
the halcyon days.

The same but changed;
the chintz is gone.
The room is smaller.

It's who was there
and what it was then
that we remember.

Leave it alone;
keep it for the hard times.
Preserve it for old age.

Do nothing to destroy it.
It's precious.

Naiya

You came at last,
already soothed and talked to.
Much loved, you brought such joy
unique and beautiful Minny Moo.
Your Mum and Dad were well prepared.
You made for four in family
and so their love increased
to welcome and enfold you.

You will grow up affirmed
by all the care that they
will take of you, by teaching you
of all in life that's good and true.

One day you'll take your leave
and fly the nest,
when all you've learned from them:
love, truth and beauty,
will stand you in good stead
in this mysterious world,
and make a purpose
for which you too can live.

Old Fashioned

He never owned a mobile phone.
He died at ninety-seven.
He always thought that when he did
that he would go to Heaven.

Descendants

When we came to live
fifty years after the war,
the First World War that is,
in the tack room
off the coachouse in the stable yard,
on a cobweb covered
moth-eaten green-baize notice board,
pinned with a single rusted thumb-tack
was a damaged photograph
of a young man
in private soldiers' uniform.
I wondered if he had children
or grandchildren in the village;
Almost certainly not.

The Tara Vie Hotel

A former friend of mine
has lunch every day
in the Tara Vie Hotel, Courtown.

If I want to see him
I go there for a chat,
Which I do, not very often.

You will have noticed
that I referred to him
as a 'former' friend.

It's not that we had a falling out.
No, our lives took different courses,
So I hadn't seen him for many years

Until one day in my early decrepitude
I happened to drop into the Tara Vie
For a spot of lunch and there he was.

We had a great chat about old times.
When we were young, life lay ahead of us
and we hadn't a care in the world.

'Do you come here often?' I asked.
'Every day for my lunch.
'The wife left me, and the family's grown and gone.

'The woman who owns the Tara Vie
'is a friend of mine'.
'Strange name' I said, 'Tara Vie'.

'Well it's like this' he said:
'It started off as the Tara View
'but the 'W' fell off early on
'and they never got round to putting it back!'

Le Petit Déjeuner

A Paris restaurant,
8.40 am on a fine June holiday morning:
we wait for breakfast.
An old man, anybody's favourite uncle,
a stick and stooped, shuffles
to a table he's sat at every morning
for more than twenty years.

As our croissants and hot chocolate arrive
we hear a commotion
two waiters kneel
beside the old man on the floor;
one loosens his shirt, the other his shoes.
In no time the siren;
an ambulance arrives.

The crew with accoutrements
to beat the band
tries to revive him.
They work away
and take it in turns
to pump his chest
without success.

One man stops,
lights a cigarette
and chats to a barman.
The old man's dead;
but they keep on trying,
knowing they'll
have to make a report
when they get back to base.

With a plethora of machines
and a bottle of oxygen
they lift the old man onto a stretcher
and into the ambulance.
Siren blaring they drive away.

We finish breakfast
and know we'll never
be back to that restaurant again.
Neither will the old man
who ate his breakfast there
for more than twenty years.

Granny In Charge

Out for a walk;
Tegan aged three:
'We forgot to clean our teeth.'
Back home: 'Naiya, take off your coat,
take off your shoes,
put on your slippers,
then you can clean your teeth.'
Naiya aged two:
'Busy day!'

The Exile

For Ian Gibson
I met a man recently I played rugby with years ago.
I didn't really play rugby with him,
for he was on the 1st XV and I was on the 3rd Z's.

I had been to the theatre and had seen his photograph
in the programme, with an introduction he had written
to the play: 'The House of Bernarda Alba.'

I was reminded of the night at a party
years ago in a flat in Adelaide Road,
when he poured a bottle of stout over my head.

I surmised that he thought I had looked lecherously
at the girl he was with, but no, this could not have been,
for I was too full in my cups to look lecherously at
anybody.

That was the last I saw of him until I picked up the
programme
in the theatre, and there he was looking out at me,
having matured into a somewhat dishevelled bohemian.

This man lives in Spain and writes significant books in
Spanish.
The best known: the definitive two-volume biography
of Lorca,
that he translated into English himself, which I find
amusing.

Sitting in the theatre before the show,
I wonder if he remembers the night he poured stout
over my head.
So I wrote to him to remind him of the incident.

Back comes a warm and friendly letter
that tells me he remembers the occasion well,
and offers a belated, fulsome and abject apology.

Sometime later the said gent arrived in Dublin for
Bloomsday.
He hadn't been in the city for more than ten years
and amongst his calls he had lunch with a former
student, the President, at the Áras.

My wife and I met him in a pub in Rathmines that no
longer exists.
We were passing a pleasant hour or so, when, looking
out the window,
he registered shock at the No 14 bus coming down the
wrong road.

It became clear to me that if you're going to live in
Spain,
write books in Spanish, and come home every ten
years,
you may be invited to lunch with the President,
but you'll certainly be out of touch with the pubs in
Rathmines,
and the route of the No 14 Bus.

The Sandwiches

I was nineteen and in hospital,
a public ward, to have my tonsils out.
(I'd strongly advise you to have
your tonsils out when you're a child.)

On the Saturday night about eight o'clock
a man in sweater and jeans
was admitted to the bed opposite me.
He had swallowed an open safety pin.

Out drinking all afternoon
he had come home to put on his good suit
to go out for a drink.

He'd been holding the safety pin in his mouth
Ready to anchor one side of his braces
When *mirabile dictu* he swallowed it.

The nurse drew the curtains
and left him standing there.
In five minutes she returned

and with an expert swish
she pulled back the curtains
and *abracadabra* there he was
sitting up in bed wearing a hospital gown.

The nurse disappeared again
and returned with a round of sandwiches
she left on his bedside locker.
'I hope you're hungry' she said
and went on down the ward.

'Holy God' said the patient
and shouted on the top of his voice:
'Nurse, nurse, there's cotton wool
 in these sandwiches.'

The nurse went to the safety pin man,
who said in a hurt and offended tone:
'The least you could'a done was
 to put on some ketchup.'

The Ascent Of Man

He looked up to the window of my bedroom,
he took out the ladder from my shed,
he climbed up to the outside of my window,
and ended up beside me in my bed.

History

Erskine Childers

A portion of St Patrick's Breastplate,
your name and dates and 'President of Ireland'
engraved upon your stone,
in a country churchyard in County Wicklow.
The ruined church, unroofed and derelict
stands sentinel among the graves of generations.

An anomaly in Irish public life;
your Protestant English background
with Irish gentry cousins,
your father a martyr of the civil war,
yourself a member of the party
and Minister of State.

I find it hard to think of you at cumann meetings;
your measured and carefully enunciated English.
But no one would deny the integrity
that did not allow you cultivate the 'cúpla focal.'
You served your day and generation creating health
boards
and doing your duty by your trust.

In course of time the people made you President;
not for you reward for work well done,
but a job to do with thoroughness
to serve the people who elected you.
You used your office to speak directly to the people.
One theme: our leisure time, our sport and recreation.

And you support your word with actions
by attending small events
in little places round the country,
and having people to the Áras,
because you knew it was important
for the President to meet the people.

Then suddenly you left us.
Our head of State, we buried you
at your own request among your cousins
in the country churchyard in County Wicklow
with ruined church, unroofed and derelict,
that stands sentinel among the graves of generations.

Mad Maxwell

He was known in the Line as Mad Maxwell;
he was mad but it just didn't matter.
He could captain his ships and they got there,
For he wasn't as mad as a hatter.

How Things Happen

If my grandfather had not left school early
and turned his hand to nothing much.
If he hadn't joined the army
And been posted to India
Where his brother who hadn't left school early
Was a surgeon in the Indian Army.
If my grandfather hadn't been with his regiment
Coming home from India
When they were ordered to Khartoum
to rescue General Gordon
who had been surrounded by the Mahdi.
If they hadn't been too late
and the Mahdi hadn't beheaded the general
and they hadn't continued home to Clonmel
where my grandfather met and married my grandmother
and if my grandfather hadn't been posted to Wexford
where he begat a girl, eight boys and died,
the sixth of whom was my father
who was left behind when his siblings had grown and gone.
If his eldest brother had not turned up in Wexford
and told my father, his bags packed for Australia,
to unpack them and stay to look after his mother.
If later that summer my father had
not gone on a walking tour in Cork,
called to see a friend and met his sister
whom two years later he married.
If he hadn't set up a small business in Wexford
Where I was born. I would not have been here
To write the foregoing.

Mahler And Paul Durcan

Here sit I on the sofa
listening to Mahler's Fifth Symphony,
reading poems by Paul Durcan.

I enjoy listening to Mahler
the best way I know how.
As I don't know much about music
I can't reconcile what I read in the CD booklet
with the music that entrances me.

'Meat and two Veg'
is how a musician friend of mine
described Mahler's Symphonies.
His music has real substance,
unlike some 'jumpy' music of Mozart.

As I don't really understand music,
I don't know what to do with my brain
when I'm listening to it,
so this morning I chose

a collection of poems by Paul Durcan,
of whom Seamus Heaney said:
'Durcan's copious bitter sweet clowning
Is a way of telling the truth slant'.

I understand that,
so if I knew more about music
perhaps I would see that Mahler
too is telling the truth slant –
without the clowning.

Good With Tomatoes

I know a widow woman
who bought a house in Dalkey,
found it wasn't what she wanted,
sold it and bought a house in Harold's Cross.
Would anyone with a tither of wit
sell a house in Dalkey
and go to live in Harold's Cross?

She was lonely living on her own
so she took in a lodger,
(that's what you do with lodgers,
you take them in),
a foreman on a building site up the road.

All was well until one night she woke
to find the lodger beside her in bed.
She ordered him to leave the bed immediately.
At breakfast she asked for his latchkey
and told him to pack his bags and go.

She had turned down a generous offer
for a gîte she had in France.
Then the crash.
Now she can't sell it for half the price.

A long standing widow
She buried her husband in the wrong grave
over which she fell out with her sister-in-law
who later that year won the lottery.

She was however good at picking
the ripest firmest tomatoes in the supermarket.

St Helen`s Bay

St Helen's Bay;
God only knows how it acquired its name
or who she was or why she came.

A long and grey deserted strand
strewn with ragged tiers of salt bleached sea wrack.
A massive boulder thirty yards to seaward,
at low tide dominates the scene,
covered at high tide but for a foot or two,
worn smooth by countless years of incessant wave
action.

Holy wells among the rocks left by a receding tide
reflect the evening sun.
A sandy bank of coarse scutch-grass
speckled with sea daisies
falls from a hinterland of barren fields
marked off by a fence of corroded netting wire.

The Former Taoiseach

A former Prime Minister of Ireland,
An Taoiseach, *as Gaeilge*,
who lost power at the last general election but one,
and never came to terms with leaving office,
killed a widow with five acres, a cow and twelve
children,
(four in America, four in England and three in Dublin;
two in the Civil Service),
behind her cottage,
down a long boreen, off a bog road,
in the north-west of County Mayo.

He is at present behind bars
in Castlebar Garda station,
waiting for charges to be preferred,
commensurate with his status in life
as a former Taoiseach.

The King Of Romania

I know a man
on speaking terms
with the King of Romania.

He minces backwards
as he tells of meeting him
a second time
at a party,
        and reminded him
of the first time they met.

However, the King of Romania
is only interested
in meeting people
who can help him
claim back his throne,
not in backward-mincing
party-going
social-climbing people,
even if they did go
to almost the right school.

Miler

One writer describes the Elizabethan Church of Ireland
as 'The Wild West of the Anglican Communion,'
and Miler McGrath its most notorious cowboy.

Miler was appointed bishop of Down and Connor by
the Pope,
and then changed horses to become Protestant Bishop
of Clogher.
A favourite of Elizabeth, she made him Archbishop of
Cashel.

Flamboyant, scandalous and little better than a
gangster,
he rode around his diocese on a horse
and terrorised clergy and people alike.

Useful to the crown, Elizabeth overlooked
that Miler had had his children baptised Catholics.
Always in rude good health, the brigand lived to be a
hundred.

His Grace Of Dublin

In the late eighteenth century,
one of the Protestant Archbishops of Dublin
was a notorious alcoholic.

The first inkling of the problem
came to light when his secretary
was settling accounts for communion wine
for his private chapel.

He then discovered the Archbishop
had secret pockets sewn into his cassock
so he wouldn't be found wanting
on even the most formal occasions.

Eventually the matter became
common knowledge in the diocese,
as the Archbishop smelled of drink
and slurred his words at public events.

He almost instituted a churchwarden as rector,
but fortunately the Archdeacon,
(who had the same problem himself),
noticed just in time.

Services in country parishes
were a particular problem when
His Grace disappeared behind the church
before and after the service.

Port was the Archbishop's favourite tipple.
At dinner parties at The Palace,
after the ladies had withdrawn,
he couldn't wait for the port to come round again,

so much so that his butler placed
a decanter for himself
on the table in front of him.

His wife, a tee-totaller, asked the butler
if he could dilute the decanter
to prevent him, (if you'll excuse the pun),
making a complete disgrace of himself.

The butler, who had become used
to covering for the Archbishop replied:
'I'm afraid not madam, His Grace
will drink only the best vintage port available.'

The end came one autumn evening,
when, late for a state occasion at The Castle,
the Archbishop fell out of his carriage.

The coachman thought he heard a thud on the way,
but didn't discover he was missing
until he opened the door in the Castle Yard,
and stood back to let the Archbishop out!

Over the years the diocese
and the civic authorities,
had learned to make allowances
for His Grace's little weakness,

but despite everything,
when he was sober
he was a very good Archbishop.

His Grace Of Armagh

One eighteenth century Archbishop of Armagh
had an expensive avocation.
He was addicted to gambling.

Although he didn't consider the afterlife a gamble,
he wouldn't have bet on it; his weakness was dice
that he played in a casino with the degenerate gentry.

Like gamblers the world over, he considered his losses
a temporary setback till his luck would turn,
but he lost badly and was crippled by debt.

Some senior clergy lent him money,
but got neither preferment
nor their money back.

He sacked the Diocesan Treasurer,
took over finance himself,
lost everything and broke the diocese.

His wife, at her wits end,
let some servants go, before one day
confronting him with her own planned departure.

In a final throw of the dice, so to speak,
His Grace rode to Termonfeckin
to touch his opposite number for a loan.

The Catholic Archbishop received him kindly,
but was strapped himself,
living in a modest house on the edge of the village.

On his way back to Armagh,
the Archbishop stopped at an inn to have,
with his last few pence, a tankard of ale,

when, by Divine intervention,
he had a heart attack
and expired on the spot.

His wife received the news with relief,
and after the funeral she moved to Tyrone,
taken in by her unmarried sister.

Belief

Old Judd

Old Judd lied.
Everyone knew he lied
but they loved his stories,
so no one said:
'I don't believe you, Judd,'
but nobody knew where
truth and fantasy met,
not even Judd.

Theologians

To Clement of Alexandria
Plato was 'The Attic Moses.'
These early theologians
knew more than one supposes.

People, Clem said,
when they get out of bed
should be models of serenity,
speak softly, laugh quietly
and certainly, burp gently.

By this attitude of quietness
and personal sobriety
he claimed the average Christian
would have more of God's society.

Origen was another
of the breed of 'theologian,'
but from Clement his master
he differed, God knows,
he thought he'd be a martyr,
but his mother hid his clothes.

Origen is determined,
so his Christian life enhances,
when he does himself a mischief
and forever ruins his chances!
If you want to get a handle on this life
and how to live it,
eschew this weird codology,
have the gumption and the common-sense
to do your own theology.

Order

What drives a man to need order,
or a woman for that matter.
Some need order like the alcoholic needs hooch
or the smoker needs weed.

How free can we be of what comes in our genes
and what sculpts us in our early years.
How far are these indelible
as we play our hand of cards?

Jesus Me

Three years of age;
where did she get the virago stance,
hands on hips, face like thunder?
'I'm the boss in this house,'

Playing with her Dad on the floor:
'Jesus me,' she exclaimed.
'You mustn't say that Tegan.'
'Is that a bad word, Daddy?'
'No, but we don't say it.'

With indignant tone
to mitigate the gravity
of her transgression:
'Well I only said it to myself.'

Fra Domenico

When they finally burned Girolamo Savonarola
they burned two other friars with him.
One was Fra Domenico della Pescia,
the purest and kindliest man in Florence.

From a small farm outside Pescia,
he left before he learned the facts of life.
On the day they lit the Bonfire of the Vanities
he was on a mission out of town.

Not that he didn't approve. He did.
He abhorred the ostentation of the rich
as much as Fra Girolamo, and spent the previous day
collecting vanities from door to door.

Fra Domenico was a man more sinned against than
sinning.
He followed blindly his mentor
without the perspicacity to understand
the political intrigue of the puritan purge.

His obsession: female dress and adornment
that might violate the sumptuary laws,
to the extent that some of his confrères said
he had an eye for the ladies, or was even transvestite.

Others said he was as gay as could be,
but whichever it was, nobody at the convent
believed he was active; latent, yes, and entirely
dormant.
Fra Domenico was as pure as the driven snow.

Some of the friars of San Marco said that
if his mentor, Fra Girolamo, became Pope,
which is what they thought he was angling for, he'd
make
Domenico head of the Congregation for Modesty and
Pure Thoughts.

When the Santa Croce Franciscans threw down a
challenge
to the San Marco Dominicans,
to decide which of them was preaching the truth,
a grand competition was planned for the Piazza della
Signoria.

A friar from each convent would walk through a fire,
and God would preserve the one that served truth,
while the other in turn would certainly burn.
This would stop chatter and settle the matter.

Like all good challenges rules were agreed,
but when Fra Domenico, the Dominican's man
wanted to enter the fire bearing the Host,
the Franciscans cried 'foul,' and all bets were off.

Now Pope Alex VI, (father of much maligned Lucrezia,
a pawn in his politics, but a lady at heart,
father too of Cesare, that detestable brigand),
was target of Savonarola's reforming crusade.

Savonarola, (also a thorn in the flesh of the powerful
Medici),
was offered a Red Hat by the Pope as a sop.
But wise to the ruse he declined, and was hanged and
then burned
along with Fra Silvestro, and the hapless Domenico.

No doubt the saintly Domenico went straight to heaven,
where to this day he looks down
on contemporary female fashion,
shocked to the core of his immortality,
by displays of feminine sartorial immorality;

It's not sumptuousness, but skimpiness
these days will offend him;
minis, bare midriffs, bikinis
and topless bottoms on beaches.
He'll be compiling a dossier of transgressions
for his Master for the Day of Judgment.

What Savonarola is up to is impossible to speculate.

Golf, Golf, Bloody Golf

They all play golf.
All my friends play golf.
The whole world, it seems, plays golf.

I met a man at a funeral
who started to tell me,
shot by shot,
hole by hole,
a round he had played that morning.

At the third hole
I stopped him.
'Do you honestly expect me to stand here,'
I said, 'and listen to you telling me,
shot by shot,
hole, by hole,
a round of golf
you played this morning,
and this poor man
stone dead in his coffin,
his widow distraught,
and his family not knowing
which end of them is up?'

At a party
a friend of mine
bored the wits out of my wife
explaining to her in detail
how after thirty years
of a perfect swing,
it had gone off;
like milk in hot weather.
He was back with the 'pro'
to have his swing corrected.

Have they no imagination?
Have they no idea
how talking golf
bores the wits out of
non-golfers?

How would they like it
if a stamp collector
cornered them in
a one way conversation
about how he tracked down
a penny black,
bought it at the right price
and rescued it for posterity
by expertly steaming it off
a damaged envelope?

I have no objection whatever
to people playing golf,
so long as,
like skeletons in the cupboard,
they keep it to themselves.
If they must,
they can bore the wits out of each other.

Two thirds of the world is starving.
There are wars everywhere,
and what, it seems,
does everyone do?
Play golf!

Golfers don't seem interested to discuss
whether there's a God or not,
or whether evolution
really was the best idea ever.
All they want to do
is play golf.
Golf, golf, bloody golf.

The Papal Nuncio

The last Papal Nuncio to Ireland,
an Italian born and bred,
was a cricket fanatic.
His previous posting had been the West Indies;
and when he enquired there about local religions,
his informant included cricket on the list.

He decided to investigate
and in no time he was hooked.
Very soon he had devised a way
to marry both his beliefs.

He spent hours incognito
at cricket matches
dressed like an upper-class English gent

to preserve his anonymity,
in order to be sure than no one
sent a report to the Vatican.

When he arrived in Ireland,
after he had presented his credentials
the first thing he asked the President was:
'Is there cricket?'

She told him there was,
as she knew that Ireland had done well
in the recent World Cup,

but since she was
a Northern Catholic
she knew nothing about the game.

The Nuncio soon briefed himself,
and could be seen in summer in civvies
watching cricket around the city.

He continued to practise the religion of his birth
and for a while he kept
both balls in the air.

He eventually went to Rome,
tendered his resignation to the Pope
and renounced his natal faith.

He returned to Ireland,
joined the Irish Cricket Union
and immersed himself in his chosen devotion.

Not long after that, one day he took ill
while watching cricket
in the Phoenix Park.

He died on the spot,
and as you might expect
he went straight to Lords.

Bruno

The Vatican has moved on.
Yesterday the Pope made a pilgrimage
to Campo dei Fiori
to pray at the statue of Giordano Bruno,
a Nolan, from Nola in the south of Italy.

James Joyce gave him an Irish identity
as an ancestor of the well-known family
of school-book publishers,
Browne and Nolan!

Burned as a heretic in 1600 AD
because of what he believed about the universe;
he had questioned church authority
to decide on such matters.

The Vatican did not reply
to enquiries from the press
as to what the Pope's prayer had been.

It really doesn't matter what he prayed;
Bruno had been ignored
by the Church for four hundred years,

and there's only one thing
worse than being reviled
and that's to be ignored.

The Man Who Knew Almost Everything

I knew a man who knew
damned well almost everything.
He died,
and I'm almost certain
that now he knows
damned well absolutely nothing.

Poetry

What Is Poetry?

I have two friends
who don't like poetry.
It's not a case of not caring for it
or not being inspired by it.
They positively abhor it.
One of them told me there were two things
he would not like to see his son turn to:
Irish dancing and poetry.
One of these friends is a scientist
and the other an IT wallah.
There are horses for courses:
you can't expect the Chief Justice
to perform a heart transplant
or a farm labourer to ice cakes.

They both say things like:
'if it doesn't rhyme and it doesn't scan
it isn't poetry anyway,'
as though that in itself settled the matter.
I didn't bother any longer to counter their carps
until recently when one of them asked:
'What is poetry for?'
as though everything had to be 'for' something,
like bicycle clips or a lump hammer.

Many of the great poets of the world
have said something about what poetry is.
None of them, as far as I know
has said what poetry is for.

The truth of the matter is,
as Kenneth Koch, a dead American poet said:
'Poetry is often regarded as a mystery.
No one is quite sure where poetry comes from,
no one is quite sure exactly what it is,
and none knows, really, how anyone is able to write it.'

So well you may ask after all that:
'What then is to be said for poetry?'
In the immortal words of the casual help
when he comes to be paid for his work:
and how much do I owe you?
'I'll leave it to yourself, Sir.'

Paul Durcan And Cricket

I sit on the sofa at 6.45 am
watching cricket on TV
with the sound turned off.
I'm reading from Paul Durcan's
latest collection of poetry,
a Christmas present to myself.

Another wicket. Another poem.

I have only one regret in life:
that I didn't play more cricket.
I read a fair deal of poetry,
but these days
much of it is barely comprehensible,
even to someone who loves poetry.

Thank goodness for Paul Durcan,
and poetry I can make sense of.
I'm also most grateful for cricket.

The Poets

With apologies to Horace; (Satires, Book 1 Satire IX)

Retired and having time to spare,
walking down Westmoreland Street,
on my way to cross the river
to call on a friend.
I was turning over in my head a few lines, totally
absorbed,
when a man, I knew only slightly,
approached me from behind.
He put his hand on my shoulder, and said:
'How's she cuttin'?'
'Fine,' I said and walked on.
He kept up with me, his hand still on my shoulder.
Wanting to forestall him I asked:
'Is there something I can do for you?'
'Listen to me. I'm something of a poet myself.'
'I'm glad to hear that,' I said,
despite trying to shake him off.
I soon began to get hot under the collar,
and wished I could be rude or even frosty
to fix this fellow.
He kept yammering on, reciting verse,
and when I failed to respond he said:
'I can see you are impatient to get rid of me.
 Where are you going? I'll just tag along.'
'I'm going to see a friend' I said,
'on the other side of the river.'
'I'm glad of the walk, so I'll come with you.

We poets must stick together.'
My heart sank and I quickened my pace.
I crossed the bridge and looked wistfully at the river.
As I walked up the quays I said:
'won't somebody be expecting you?'
'Nobody in the whole wide world,' he said.
'My family don't talk to me,
nor do any of my friends.'
'A wonder.' I thought to myself,
and then suddenly I remembered
what my mother had told me years ago.
On the Saturday after I was born
'Biddy Behind the Hill' called to the house
when she was in town for her groceries.
Having put a coin in my hand
She said to my mother:
'This young man will not die of a heart attack,
nor of TB nor pneumonia or pleurisy,
nor any disease known to doctors.
Some day someone will talk him to death.
If he's wise he'll keep his distance from talkative
people.'
As we approached the Four Courts 'the poet' said:
'I'm due inside there at two o'clock;
I'm bringing my neighbour to court for nuisance.
Will you hang around and support me?
A person of your standing would count.'
'I'm late as it is.' I said, 'I must go.'
'Then I'll stick with you and let the case drop.'
'I don't think that's the right decision,' I said.
We kept on up the quays.

'Which faction do you belong to?' he asked.
'Which faction of what?'
'To which gang of poets do you belong?'
'I don't belong to any gang.
Whoever mugs you it won't be a gang of poets.'
Just then I saw my friend approaching.
I could see he read the situation perfectly.
I was impatient for him to say something to rescue me.
He kept smiling but uttered
no word of escape.
Making facial gestures I tugged at his sleeve.
I nodded and winked,
but he pretended not to understand.
Furious , I said:
'Haven't we business to transact.'
'Yes but it can wait to another time.
This is Ash Wednesday,
and I don't want to prevent anyone's penance.'
'I'm not religious,' I said.
'Well I am,' he replied, 'it's a weakness I share
with most of humanity.'
With that he disappeared into the crowd.
Just then, 'the poet' spotted his neighbour accused.
His blood boiled and he shouted across:
'I'll see you in court.'
He turned on his heel and left me,
and with that I was saved.